SPACE

Sun, Moon and Stars

by Sally Hewitt

Aladdin/Watts
London • Sydney

THE NIGHT SKY

Binoculars

Look up at the **night sky**. You can see the Moon and thousands of tiny twinkling lights.

It is difficult to see what is in the **night sky** because everything is so far away. Binoculars or a telescope help us to see more clearly.

The night sky

The best place to look at the **night sky** is on a hill, away from bright city lights. There are many different objects in the **night sky**.

Moon
The Moon is a ball of rock moving round the Earth.

Stars
Stars are balls of burning gas.

Planets
Planets are balls of rock and gas.

Comets
Comets are melting lumps of space ice and dust.

Galaxies
A galaxy is a group of billions of stars.

Satellites
Satellites are spacecraft.

EARTH AND SPACE

The **Earth** is the planet we live on. It is a big rock spinning in **space**.

Pictures taken from **space** show that the **Earth** is shaped like a ball. It looks blue because it is mostly covered in water.

The Earth has air, water, heat and light – all the things plants and animals need to live and grow.

The Earth

Space is the Sun, the Moon, the planets, the stars and all the empty space between them.

The **Earth** has a layer of air around it -- the atmosphere. This air gets thinner and thinner, the higher you go. In **space**, there is no air at all!

An astronaut in space

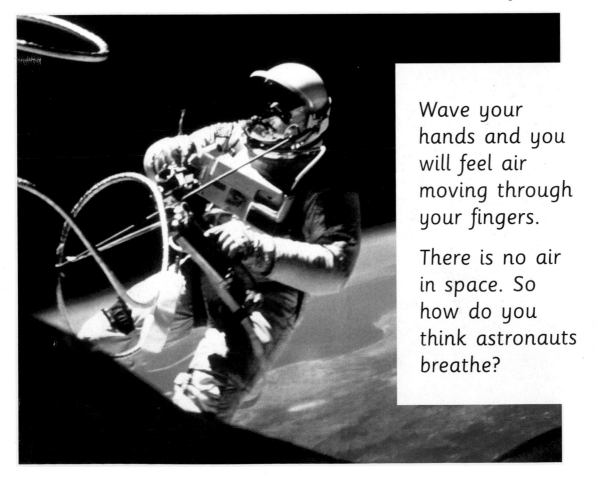

Wave your hands and you will *feel* air moving through your fingers.

There is no air in space. So how do you think astronauts breathe?

MOON AND SUN

The nearest space object to the Earth is the **Moon**. It is a ball of rock moving round the Earth.

The **Moon** has no light of its own. Moonlight is really sunlight bouncing off the **Moon**.

As it moves, the **Moon** seems to change shape. We only see the part of the **Moon** lit up by the **Sun**.

The Moon

You can see dark patches on the Moon, called seas. But there is no water on the Moon. There is no air either.

Why can't anything live on the Moon?

The **Sun** is the nearest star to the Earth.
It is a giant ball of fiery gas that
gives us heat and light.

There would be no life
on the Earth without the **Sun**.

The Earth spins in space but the
Sun stays in the same place.

As Earth spins, it looks as though
the **Sun** is moving across the sky.

THE SOLAR SYSTEM

The Sun is much bigger than the Earth. If the Sun was a basketball then Earth would be the size of a grain of rice.

The Earth's gravity pulls us back to the ground when we jump into the air.

Very large objects like the Sun pull things towards them. This pull is called **gravity**.

Gravity makes planets, moons, rocks, dust and ice move round and round the Sun. We say they orbit the Sun.

Neptune   **Uranus**   **Saturn**

Everything that orbits the Sun is part of the **solar system**.

Eight planets are in our **solar system**. The Earth is the only planet with plants and animals. It is just the right distance from the Sun for life to exist.

The other planets are all too hot, too cold, or do not have air to breathe.

Which of the planets would be too hot for us to live on?

Which would be too cold?

Jupiter   Mars   Earth   Venus   Mercury   Sun

MERCURY, VENUS AND MARS

Mercury is the closest planet to the Sun. It is so near the Sun it is much hotter than an oven.

Venus is the second planet. It is completely covered in thick, yellow clouds.

You can spot **Mercury** and **Venus** in the early evening or early morning.

Venus is the brightest object in the night sky.

Mars

The Earth is the third planet from the Sun.

Mars, the fourth planet, is half the size of Earth. It looks red because it is covered in red dust.

The surface of Mars

The planets have no light of their own. Like the Moon, they are lit up by the Sun.

Shine a torch onto a football in a dark room. See how the torch lights up one side of the ball.

THE OUTER PLANETS

Jupiter, Saturn, Uranus and **Neptune** are the furthest planets from the Sun. They are enormous balls of gas.

Jupiter is the biggest planet. It has more than 60 moons.

The red spot on Jupiter is a giant hurricane that is three times as big as Earth!

Jupiter

Saturn is the second largest planet. It is surrounded by colourful rings of rock and dust.

Uranus and **Neptune** look greenish blue. They both have rings and moons.

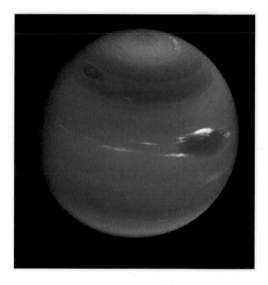

Neptune

You can see Jupiter's moons and Saturn's rings through a strong telescope or binoculars.

A tripod holds the telescope steady. Why do a telescope or binoculars need to be steady?

15

Stars moving across the sky

STARS

Stars are enormous, very hot balls of gas, just like the Sun. They look like tiny lights twinkling in the sky because they are so far away.

The **stars** seem to move slowly across the night sky. But it is Earth that is spinning round and round in space.

16

The brightest **stars** make patterns in the sky called **constellations**. You can learn to spot **stars** and know their names.

Star-gazing

The **stars** look near to each other although they are very far apart.

The constellation of Orion can be seen from anywhere on Earth.

Look for the seven bright stars that make up Orion's shoulders, belt and feet.

Orion

GALAXIES, METEORS AND COMETS

Galaxy

Our solar system belongs to a very large group of stars called a **galaxy**.

There are many **galaxies** in space. Each one is made up of billions of stars, planets, gas and dust.

The galaxy we belong to is called The Milky Way.

On a clear night, it looks like a milky path of stars across the sky.

Galaxies also contain smaller objects that fly through space: **asteroids, meteors** and **comets.**

Asteroids are big chunks of rock and metal. Millions of **asteroids** orbit the Sun between Mars and Jupiter.

Meteors are bits of space dust and rock.

As they fall through Earth's atmosphere they burn up and look like shooting stars.

Asteroid Gaspra

Comets are big balls of ice and dirt. When a comet flies near the Sun it starts to melt. Gas and dust stream out behind it in a long tail.

Comet

SPACE TRAVEL

Astronauts are people who travel in space. They have to take air to breathe and all the food and water they need for their journey.

Powerful rockets blast spacecraft away from Earth into space.

Some **astronauts** have landed on the Moon, but so far, no one has landed on a planet.

An astronaut on the Moon

A **space shuttle** is a spacecraft that can be used again and again. It carries **astronauts** on space missions that last about a week.

Space shuttle

Some **astronauts** work in a **space station** in orbit around Earth. A **space shuttle** can land and take off from it.

Space station

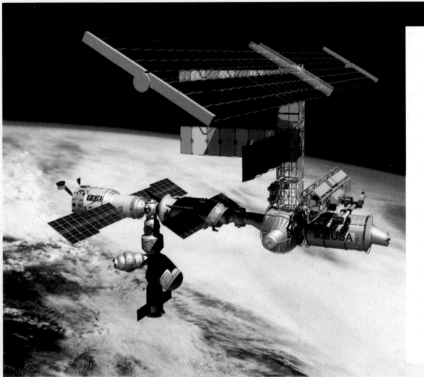

One day, people will be able to travel farther into space.

Plan a trip of the places in space you would like to visit.

21

EXPORING SPACE

We learn about what is in space from
scientists called **astronomers**.

Space telescope

The Hubble
Space Telescope
orbits the Earth.
It can see a
very long way
into space.

They look deep into space
using giant **telescopes**.

Some **telescopes** are high
on mountains where the
air is clear.

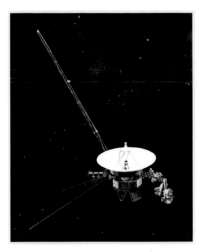

Voyager 2

Robot

Spacecraft have been sent into space to explore the planets.

Voyager 2 has been right to the edge of the solar system. It has visited Saturn, Uranus, Neptune and Pluto.

We cannot send spacecraft to stars because the stars are too far away.

Two robots are exploring Mars. If there is water on Mars, there could be life there too! Draw a picture of what might live on the hot, dusty, red planet Mars.

JOURNEY INTO SPACE

Look out for words about space.

"It's a clear night," said Dad.
"Great for looking at the stars."

"Can we look at the stars too?"
asked Anand and Leyla.
"All right," said Dad.
"We'll go to the park,
away from the street lights."

"I'll get binoculars and a torch,"
said Anand.

They looked up into space.
"It's a full Moon tonight," said Dad.

"I can see dark patches,"
said Leyla.

"They are called seas," said
Dad, "but they are really
plains and craters. There's
no water on the Moon."

24

"What's that big, bright star next to the Moon?" asked Anand.
"It's not a star, it's the planet Jupiter," said Dad.

"Where's Mars?" asked Leyla.
"We can't see Mars now," said Dad.
"Why not?" asked Anand.

"Because Earth and all the planets are moving round the Sun," said Dad.

"They orbit the Sun," said Leyla.

"That's right. And Earth is spinning in space. We need a star chart to tell us when and where to find stars and planets."

"I wish I could go on a journey into space," said Leyla.

"I'll take you," said Dad. "Put on your space-suits!"

"Get into the spacecraft and fire the rockets," said Anand.

"10, 9, 8, 7, 6, 5, 4, 3, 2, 1... BLAST OFF!" they all shouted.

"First stop, the Sun!" said Leyla. "No, it's too hot. It'll burn us up!" said Anand.

"We'll miss out Mercury and Venus too," said Dad. "They're too near the Sun."

"There's the Moon," said Leyla. "Let's take a closer look at those craters and seas."

"The other side of the Moon is always dark. We never see it from Earth," said Dad.

"Here comes Mars! Uh, oh! Watch out for those asteroids. One nearly smashed into us!" said Dad. "I can see Jupiter. Count its moons."

"I counted 16!" said Anand. "Saturn next. Its rings are all the colours of the rainbow."

"There go Uranus and Neptune!" said Dad.

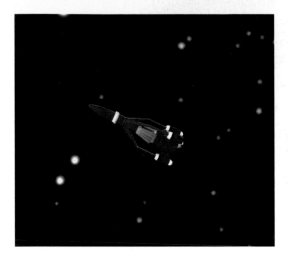

"That was quick!" said Leyla.

"Yes, but it would take years and years for a real spacecraft to travel to Neptune," said Anand.

"Now we're deep in space. It's dark and empty here," said Dad. "We're going to our nearest star, Proxima Centauri."

"Are we nearly there yet?" asked Leyla.

Dad laughed. "Nearly. Watch out for comets and alien spacecraft!"

"Aliens don't exist!" said Anand.

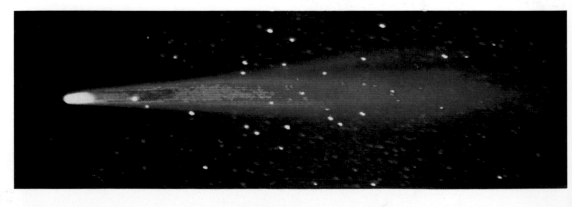

"They do! I just saw one, but you missed him!" said Leyla.

"Now we're heading for the edge of our galaxy," said Dad.

"The Milky Way," said Anand and Leyla together.
"So is that the end of space?" asked Leyla.

"No," said Dad. "Space goes on and on and on.
There are many, many more galaxies.
Each one has billions of stars and planets."

"And moons and asteroids," said Anand.
"And aliens!" said Leyla.

"Maybe," said Dad.
"We don't know. We'd better get back to Earth now. It's time for bed."

Dad, Anand and Leyla walked
back though the park.
A silver streak of light
shot across the sky.

"A shooting star!" cried Leyla.
"Make a wish," said Dad.

"It's not a shooting star. It's a
bit of burning space dust," said
Anand. "But it's a very beautiful
bit of space dust!" said Dad.

NIGHT SKY CHART. Get to know the night sky where
you live. Use a star chart to help you. Keep a record
of the things you see. Make a chart listing space
objects in groups. Or write your own space story!

Moon	Stars	Planets	Constellations	Other
Full	Pole Star	Venus	Orion	Shooting star
Crescent	Sirius	Jupiter	Great Bear	Satellite
Half	Vega		Libra	Milky Way
			Capricorn	

QUIZ

What four things does planet **Earth** have that animals and plants need to live and grow?

Answer on page 6

How many **planets** are in the **solar system**? Can you name them in order?

Answers on pages 10 and 11

What is a **galaxy**? What **galaxy** does the **Sun** belong to?

Answers on page 18

Which of these space objects is a star, a constellation, a comet or a planet?

Answers on pages 5, 12, 17, 19

INDEX